COUNTRIES IN OUR WORLD

KENYA
IN OUR WORLD

Ali Brownlie Bojang

A$^+$

Smart Apple Media

Published by Smart Apple Media
P.O. Box 3263, Mankato, Minnesota 56002

Printed in the United States of America at Corporate
Graphics, in North Mankato, Minnesota.

Published by arrangement with the Watts Publishing
Group LTD, London.

Library of Congress Cataloging-in-Publication Data
Brownlie Bojang, Ali, 1949-
  Kenya in our world / by Ali Brownlie Bojang.
     p. cm. -- (Countries in our world)
  Includes bibliographical references and index.
  Summary: "Describes the geography, landscape,
economy, government, and culture of Kenya today
and discusses Kenya's influence of and relations with
the rest of the world"--Provided by publisher.
  ISBN 978-1-59920-391-1 (library binding)
  1. Kenya--Juvenile literature. I. Title.
  DT433.522.B775 2012
  967.6204'3--dc22
                              2010035505

Produced for Franklin Watts by
White-Thomson Publishing Ltd
Series consultant: Rob Bowden
Editor: Sonya Newland
Designer: Amy Sparks
Picture researcher: Amy Sparks

Picture Credits
Corbis: 5 (Hulton-Deutsch Collection), 6 (Antony
Njuguna/Reuters), 11 (Micheline Pelletier), 12 (Wendy
Stone), 18 (Patrice Latron), 21 (Noor Khamis/Reuters),
26 (epa), 29 (Thomas Mukoya/Reuters); **Dreamstime:**
1 (Ajn), 8 (Aureli), 9 (Eric Isselée), 10 (Alan Ward),
14 (Jkfoto), 28 (Temistocle Lucarelli); **EASI-Images:** 7
(Rob Bowden); **Fotolia:** 23 (Eric Isselée); **Getty Images:**
15, 24 (National Geographic); **iStock:** 13, 17 (Adam
Kurt); **Photoshot:** 22 (NHPA); **Shutterstock:** 16
(Cecilia Lim H M), 19 (Rachael Russell), 25 (Lexan);
UN Photo: 20 (Milton Grant), 27 (Jorge Aramburu).
Map artwork on page 4 by Stefan Chabluk.

1305
3-2011

9 8 7 6 5 4 3 2 1

Contents

Introducing Kenya

Kenya is famous for its great natural beauty, which attracts visitors from all over the world, and it is one of Africa's main centers of banking and business. Although it suffers from poverty and civil unrest, Kenya is still one of Africa's most stable countries.

Where in the World?

Kenya lies on the equator in East Africa. Although it is largely surrounded by land, it borders the Indian Ocean in the southeast. The ports along the coastline provide a gateway for trade and travel in this part of the African continent. In the west, where Kenya meets Tanzania and Uganda, lies Lake Victoria. Sudan and Ethiopia are situated to the north, and to the east is Somalia.

Historical Global Links

Throughout its long history, Kenya has had connections with other countries. Around the seventh century, Arab traders set up towns along the Kenyan coast, and travelers came from as far away as China and Persia (now Iran). Although Arab influences declined in the 19th century, they are still evident today, particularly in Kenya's large Muslim population.

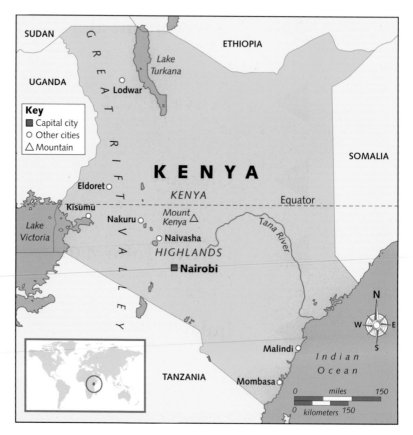

▶ *Kenya has land borders with Ethiopia to the north, Somalia to the east, Tanzania to the south, Uganda to the west and Sudan to the northwest.*

The British in Kenya

The British began to arrive in Kenya in the 18th century, and by 1895 Britain ruled the country. Many British people came to live in Kenya, particularly in the west of the country in an area known as the Highlands. They established farms to grow tea and coffee. Thousands of local people, particularly the Maasai and Kikuyu tribes, were forced off their land by the new settlers. Using Kenyan and Asian workers, the British built railways to link the heart of the country to the coast and the ports, so that goods could be sent back to Britain. By 1920, there were 9,000 European settlers living in Kenya.

IT STARTED HERE

Human Ancestors

In many parts of Kenya, scientists have found the remains of ape-like creatures believed to be very early ancestors of human beings. The earliest of these—fossils dating back more than 4.2 million years—have been discovered around the shores of Lake Turkana. Modern humans are believed to have originated here around 200,000 years ago.

▼ *Kenyans working on the building of a railway during the period of British rule.*

Independence

The British ruled Kenya for 67 years. Thousands of Kenyan soldiers fought for the British during World War I (1914–18), and they also fought in World War II (1939–45) in countries as far away as Burma. In the 1950s, some Kenyans—particularly members of the Kikuyu tribe—began to rebel against British rule. At first the British fought against the rebellion and imprisoned its leaders. Later, though, the British gave in to pressure and in 1963, Kenya became an independent country. Jomo Kenyatta, who had been involved in the Mau Mau rebellion, became the country's first president.

FAMOUS KENYAN

Ngugi wa Thiong'o (b. 1938)

Ngugi wa Thiong'o is one of Kenya's best-known writers. His most famous book, *Weep Not, Child*, was the first book by an East African to be written in English. It is about the Mau Mau rebellion—the fight by the Kikuyu people against British rule in the 1950s. In later years, Ngugi wa Thiong'o taught at universities in the United Kingdom and the United States.

Kenya Today

Kenya is famous for its stunning scenery and is one of Africa's top tourist destinations. Its game parks, mountains, and beautiful beaches are popular with visitors from all over the world. It has also recently gained fame as the birthplace of the father of Barack Obama, the president of the United States.

◀ *Traditional dancers perform at a celebration in Nairobi commemorating Kenyan independence.*

▲ *The Bamburi cement depot at the port of Mombasa. Kenya's ports are vital for importing and exporting goods to and from East Africa.*

African Leader

Today Kenya plays a leading role in areas such as trade and politics in Africa. Kenyan troops take part in peacekeeping missions in the neighboring countries of Somalia and Sudan where there are civil wars. Other neighboring countries, such as landlocked Ethiopia and Uganda, rely on Kenya's ports and roads to transport goods all over the world.

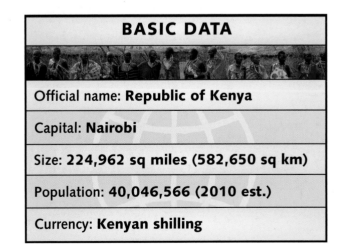

BASIC DATA

Official name: Republic of Kenya

Capital: Nairobi

Size: 224,962 sq miles (582,650 sq km)

Population: 40,046,566 (2010 est.)

Currency: Kenyan shilling

Landscapes and Environment

Kenya can be split into three main regions, each with its own landscape and climate. These range from snow-capped mountains to sandy beaches, fertile farmland to barren deserts, and open grasslands to lakes.

PLACE IN THE WORLD

Total area: **224,962 sq miles (582,650 sq km)**

Percentage of world land area: **0.39%**

World ranking: **48th**

The Northeast Region

The northeast region of Kenya is very dry and hot with sparse grassland known as the savannah. Thorn bushes and the occasional baobab tree grows here, but very little else. Not many people live in this area. Those that do are mainly nomadic—people who keep cattle, goats, or camels, and move from one feeding place to another to find the best land for grazing.

▼*Herdsmen are the main inhabitants of Kenya's dry northern regions. This area suffers from droughts, so it is not ideal for farming or human settlement.*

The Coast

Kenya's coastline stretches for 333 miles (536 km) along the southeast of the country. Here there are beautiful beaches lined with coral reefs. The climate is hot and humid all year. The beaches are popular with tourists, who also enjoy the fishing and water sports.

▲ *Malindi is one of the largest coastal towns in Kenya. It attracts thousands of tourists every year who go there to enjoy the warm weather and white-sand beaches.*

The Highlands

The area known as the Highlands lies in the southwest of the country. This region is a large plateau of rolling grassland, ranging from 3,000 to 10,000 feet (900 to 3,000 m) high. Most of the farms in Kenya have been established here because the soil is fertile, there is much rain, and the temperatures are cool at this altitude. Most of the population of Kenya lives in the Highlands, and it is home to the capital, Nairobi.

IT'S A FACT!

The Great Rift Valley is an enormous valley where the earth's crust weakened and slowly tore itself apart 20 million years ago. The valley runs right through Kenya. In total, the valley stretches 3,700 miles (6,000 km) from as far north as Syria to Malawi in the south of Africa.

9

Rivers

Most of Kenya's rivers and small lakes dry up during the dry season. This leads to water shortages all over the country. The Tana River is the largest in the country, flowing 440 miles (708 km) into the Indian Ocean. The waters of Lake Victoria, the second largest freshwater lake in the world, feed into the White Nile in Uganda. Lake Victoria also has shores in Tanzania and Uganda, linking Kenya to these countries.

THE HOME OF...

Mount Kenya

Mount Kenya is the highest mountain in Kenya and the second highest in Africa after Mount Kilimanjaro. It stands 17,057 feet (5,199 m) high and is actually an extinct volcano. The rivers that flow down Mount Kenya, including the Tana, are an important water source for the people of Kenya.

National Parks and Game Parks

Kenya has two national parks that have been declared UNESCO World Heritage Sites—Lake Turkana National Park and Mount Kenya National Park. In total, Kenya has 65 national parks and reserves. Maasai Mara is one of the world's most famous national parks, and it is estimated that every year between May and July, 1.3 million wildebeests and 400,000 zebras migrate here from Tanzania in search of water. Other animals found in Kenya include lions, antelopes, elephants, leopards, cheetahs, hyenas, rhinos, and giraffes.

◀ *The "Great Migration" sees wildebeests and zebras move between the Serengeti National Park in Tanzania and Maasai Mara in Kenya. Predators such as lions and hyenas follow the herds.*

▲ *Wangari Muta Maathai (center) with members of the Green Belt Movement, which tries to reverse the damage caused by deforestation.*

Environmental Issues

Kenya faces many environmental problems. Water pollution in the cities is caused by overcrowded shanty towns and factories. In the countryside, it is caused by the use of pesticides and fertilizers on the land. More than half of Kenya's forests have been cut down in the last 100 years, leading to soil erosion of the unprotected land. Efforts are now being made to address these issues by educating the people on the damage caused by pollution, and by encouraging more environmentally friendly farming and water management.

Population and Migration

Kenya's population is made up of both people who have always lived in the area and those who have traveled from other parts of Africa such as Sudan, Ethiopia, and Somalia. There are also people who have come from Europe, the Middle East, and Asia over hundreds of years.

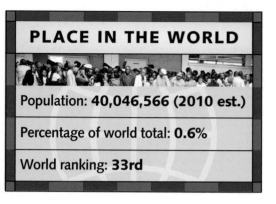

PLACE IN THE WORLD

Population: **40,046,566 (2010 est.)**

Percentage of world total: **0.6%**

World ranking: **33rd**

Kenya's Population

Although about 97 percent of Kenyans are of African descent, there are small groups of Indians, Arabs, and Europeans, particularly in the towns and cities. The number of people in Kenya has grown from about 6.5 million in 1950 to today's population of around 40 million. However, the rate at which the population is growing has dropped dramatically. Better healthcare means that parents are more confident that their children will survive, so they have smaller families. The drop in Kenya's birth rate is also due to the high number of people who die from the HIV/AIDS virus.

▼ *AIDS orphans from the Kibera slum in Nairobi are given food by community workers. The children are also educated about HIV/AIDS.*

IT'S A FACT!

Nearly half of the orphans in Kenya have been left without parents because of HIV/AIDS. In 2008, there were 1.3 million children in Kenya who had lost one or both of their parents to HIV/AIDS. That's the third highest number in the world.

Where Do Kenyans Live?

Seventy-five percent of Kenyans live in the region between Nairobi and the Ugandan border. This covers only 10 percent of the country's land area. Other groups live along the coast in the cities of Mombasa and Malindi. Most of the remaining country is too dry or too rugged for many people to live there.

Nairobi

Around 3 million people live in Nairobi, Kenya's capital city. This is the most populated city in East Africa and the 13th largest on the continent. Nairobi is the main business center in Kenya, and many international companies have their African headquarters there including Coca-Cola, Citibank, Toyota, and Google. One of the four international headquarters of the United Nations is also located in Nairobi.

▲ *An early-morning ferry is crowded with locals on their way to work in Mombasa, Kenya's second largest city.*

Moving to the City

Nairobi is a vibrant and modern city. Cities attract young people from the country who feel they can earn more money and find better career opportunities. About one-third of Kenya's population lives in urban areas. Unemployment in cities is very high, though, and more than half of Nairobi's population (around two million people) live in overcrowded shanty towns. The conditions they live in are sometimes worse than those in the villages they have left behind.

▼ *From the air, Nairobi looks like many modern cities with skyscrapers and office blocks. On the outskirts, though, are slums housing thousands of people.*

GOING GLOBAL

There are about 100,000 Kenyan Asians, most of whom live in Nairobi and Mombasa. Asians have lived in East Africa for over 100 years, coming in significant numbers during the period of British rule. Some came to work on the building of the railways. In 1968, about 70,000 fled to the UK after the Kenyan government refused to grant them work permits and licenses for their businesses.

▲ *The Yara market in Kisumu, part of the Millennium Villages program, sells local produce and crafts, helping the villagers to support themselves.*

GLOBAL LEADER

Millennium Villages

Sauri, in western Kenya, is one of the first Millennium Villages. The Millennium Villages were started by the United Nations as part of the Millennium Development Goals to help poor villages work their way out of poverty with support from governments and foreign aid. Villages such as Sauri are models for villages all over the world to follow.

Leaving Kenya

Many Kenyans who can find jobs abroad leave for what they hope will be a better life. These non-resident Kenyans find jobs in the United States, the Middle East, Europe, and Asia. Many Kenyans who live abroad send money back to their families. This is an important source of income for Kenyans back home. In 2008, an estimated US$600 million was sent to Kenya in the form of these "remittances," the equivalent of nearly four percent of all Kenyan national income.

Refugees

Kenya has long been a refuge for people from neighboring countries such as Sudan and Somalia. More than a quarter of a million refugees live in three overcrowded camps in the dry northeastern region of Kenya—one of the world's largest refugee settlements. Some Kenyans have become refugees in other countries, too. In 2008, there was violence after the presidential elections, and more than 6,000 Kenyans fled to Uganda.

Culture and Lifestyles

There are 42 different ethnic groups in Kenya, each with its own language, music, dance, and art. Most people see themselves as Kenyan, as well as a member of their ethnic group.

▼ *The Samburu people are a semi-nomadic tribe from north-central Kenya. Here, Samburu men perform a traditional dance.*

Ethnic Groups

Kenya's largest ethnic group—at 22 percent of the population—is the Kikuyu. Traditionally they were farmers, and many of them still are. However, in modern urban Kenya they also dominate business and politics. Other ethnic groups include the Luhya (14 percent), Luo (13 percent), Kalenjin (12 percent), Kamba (11 percent), Kisii, and Meru (6 percent each). Only one percent of Kenya's population is made up of Asian, European, or Arab people.

IT'S A FACT!

Swahili is a Bantu language (its proper name is KiSwahili), but about 35 percent of it is made up of Arabic words. It also has words from German, Portuguese, Indian, English, and French, due to contact in the past with all these different groups of people. It is Africa's most widely spoken African language with 50 million speakers across East Africa and the Democratic Republic of the Congo.

Traditional and Modern Lifestyles

About two-thirds of Kenyans still live in the countryside. Although there have been many changes to life in rural areas over the centuries, some aspects of tribal lifestyles have remained the same. The nomads of the north, such as the Turkana, Pokot, and Samburu peoples, measure their wealth by the number of cattle they own. The Maasai are famous for selling their jewelry and cloth. However, life in the cities is similar to that in cities in many Western countries. There are shopping malls, supermarkets, and fast-food restaurants. People work in modern offices and pass time in Internet cafés and coffee shops.

▲ *In contrast to the traditional market places found in rural areas, city residents shop in modern, air-conditioned supermarkets.*

Music

Music is a good example of how the traditional mixes with the modern in Kenya. *Benga* is a form of music that combines jazz with local music, and usually features drums, rattles, and shakers. International artists such as Sean Paul, Akon, Shaggy, and Morgan Heritage have all performed in Kenya and have many fans there. Hip-hop and R&B music are very popular. Kenyan stars often mix Swahili and English with tribal languages in their songs.

Food

Kenyan food has been influenced by other countries. On the coast—an area with strong Arabian and Indian influences—people enjoy curries and spicy food. This kind of food is also popular in the towns and cities. In rural areas, the staple food is *ugali*, a dish of mashed corn. When the family can afford it, *ugali* is eaten with a stew of beef or goat, although more usually with a vegetable stew. In the countryside and the shanty towns, people will gather around a large single bowl to eat. Wealthier Kenyans eat at expensive restaurants or take home hamburgers or pizza.

◀ *Fruit and vegetables grow well in the Kenyan climate and are staples of Kenyan cooking.*

Religion

People in Kenya are free to follow whatever religion they choose. More than 75 percent of Kenyans are Christian. Ten percent are Muslims and another 10 percent are classified as having indigenous beliefs, based on their tribal group. Many people combine different beliefs in their religion. For example, a Christian or a Muslim may also hold indigenous African beliefs.

THE HOME OF...

The Safari Rally

Kenya's Safari Rally is considered to be the toughest cross-country car rally in the world. It is a two-day race through the Kenyan bush. Drivers have to contend with wild animals and potholed roads. Rally drivers from all over the world take part.

▲ *Kenyan runner Sammy Wanjiru (third from the right) won the London Marathon in 2009 in the fastest time ever—2 hours, 5 minutes, and 10 seconds. He also won the marathon at the 2008 Olympics.*

Sports

Kenyans love sports—especially soccer, which is the most popular one to watch and play. The British introduced the game of cricket in 1896 and this is quite popular, too. However, Kenya is probably most famous for its record-breaking long-distance runners. Because they train at such high altitudes, Kenyan runners have an advantage over other athletes.

GOING GLOBAL

Many Kenyan athletes have changed their nationality following bids from rich countries in the Middle East. Their positive international reputation means they are offered money and other benefits to represent these countries in competitions, and they often change their names to Arabic ones. As a result, Kenyan athletes are improving their adopted countries' sporting reputations.

Economy and Trade

Kenya is one of the wealthiest countries in Africa. It is a vital center of finance, transportation, and business for all of East Africa. Despite this, half of its population lives on less than US$1 a day. The global economic crisis that began in 2008 has slowed the rate of Kenya's economic growth.

IT'S A FACT!

Kenya has particularly close ties with its neighbors, Tanzania and Uganda. Together these countries established the East African Community, an organization set up to help these countries cooperate and trade with each other. In 2007, Burundi and Rwanda joined the Community as full members.

The Farming Industry

Farming is still the most important part of the Kenyan economy. Seventy-five percent of the workforce is involved in farming, but only 12 percent of them are involved in growing cash crops (crops grown especially for export). The rest are small farmers who grow just enough crops such as beans, cassava, corn, and potatoes to feed their families.

▼ *Tea-pickers work on a plantation in Limuru, central Kenya. Tea and coffee plantations were established here during the period of British rule.*

Cash Crops

Cash crops are responsible for more than 50 percent of Kenya's export earnings. Growing vegetables, herbs, spices, and flowers for export is big business. Kenya is Africa's leading producer of tea and fourth in the world behind India, China, and Sri Lanka. Coffee is also an important export, and is found in supermarkets and coffee shops all over the United States and Europe. Other farming exports include tobacco, sugar, and cotton. Sugar and cotton production have suffered in recent years as world prices have dropped and other countries have been able to produce them cheaper.

GOING GLOBAL

Kenya produces 31 percent of Europe's cut flowers, such as roses and carnations, and the flower-growing industry employs at least 500,000 Kenyans. However, growing flowers uses up precious water supplies and takes up land that could be used for growing food crops. To make sure the flowers arrive fresh they are transported by air, which has a negative impact on the environment. Some people argue that flowers flown from Africa use less energy overall than those produced in Europe because they are not grown in heated greenhouses.

▲ *A worker at a flower farm in Naivasha pushes a cart of red roses ready to be exported to Europe in time for Valentine's Day.*

Tourism

Tourism is the industry that brings the most foreign income into Kenya. It is responsible for 15 percent of Kenya's gross domestic product, or GDP—the value of everything that Kenya produces. In 2007, more than one million tourists visited Kenya. Tourism is a growing industry, but it is not developing as quickly as it might. People are often afraid to travel to Kenya, because there have been terrorist attacks and riots. There are other countries in Africa, especially South Africa, that have attractions similar to those in Kenya, so tourists may choose to go there instead if the situation in Kenya is not made more stable.

▲ *The main tourist attractions in Kenya are wildlife safaris where people are taken on tours across the savanna to see animals such as lions and elephants.*

IT'S A FACT!

China has taken an interest in oil exploration in Africa, and the Kenyan government has given the China National Offshore Oil Company exclusive rights to look for oil in the Mandera area of northeast Kenya. China now controls 28 percent of the total area in Kenya set aside for oil exploration.

PLACE IN THE WORLD

Value of economy: **US$30,236,000**

Percentage of world total: **0.05%**

World ranking: **82nd**

▼ *The debt built up by the Kenyan government puts a strain on the economy and means that many Kenyan children grow up in poverty.*

Corruption

Kenya is wealthier than most African countries, and it has the potential to be an economically successful country. However, it has suffered some setbacks. This has mainly been caused by the corruption of government officials who took money for doing business only with certain people. This corruption gave Kenya a bad reputation around the world. Although efforts have been made to stop corruption, the reforms have not been very successful, and the problem is still widespread.

Debt

Under former president Daniel arap Moi, Kenya built up huge debts that now stand at nearly US$7 billion. This means that Kenya must pay back huge amounts of money to wealthier countries in debt repayments every year, which puts a great strain on the country's economy.

Government and Politics

Kenya is a republic, which means that it is not ruled by a king or queen, but by a government elected by the people. The president is the head of the government. Elections are held at least every five years to choose a president and members of parliament.

All Pull Together

When Jomo Kenyatta became president in 1963, he wanted to build a new Kenya. He hoped to create a united country based on the Swahili word *Harambee*, which means "all pull together." To start, he allowed other political parties to exist in Kenya—just like in the United States. But by 1969, Kenyatta had banned all other parties. His political party was the only one allowed, and he had all the power. Even after Kenyatta died in 1978, his successor, Daniel arap Moi, continued to rule in the same way. Western countries began to pressure the Kenyan government to make politics more fair, and in 1991, other political parties were allowed again.

FAMOUS KENYAN

Jomo Kenyatta (1894–1978)

Jomo Kenyatta is known as the father of the Kenyan nation. As a member of the Kikuyu tribe, he campaigned in the UK and Russia for Kikuyu land rights. He founded the Pan-African Federation in 1946 with Kwame Nkrumah of Ghana. In 1960, Kenyatta became leader of KANU, the Kenyan African National Union, while imprisoned by the British. He became Kenya's first president in 1963.

▼ *Jomo Kenyatta was the first president of an independent Kenya.*

The Kenyan Parliament

The Kenyan parliament is known as the National Assembly (or *Bunge*), and it has 210 members elected by the people. The president chooses 12 members. Kenya also has a system of local government. The country is divided into eight provinces and each of these has a commissioner who reports to the president. To win the presidency, a candidate needs to get 25 percent of the total votes in at least five of Kenya's eight provinces.

▲ *Nairobi's City Hall is the center of local government for the province of Nairobi. Local governments make decisions about issues such as healthcare and education.*

IT'S A FACT!

Kenya is a member of several international groups, including the United Nations, the Commonwealth, the African Union, the World Trade Organization, and the East African Community. Membership of organizations like these means that Kenya has a say about important issues that affect countries worldwide.

Political Unrest

An election was held in 2007, but after the winner had been announced, there were riots and violence. Many people believed the election had been rigged in favor of the president, Mwai Kibaki, and this was another example of political corruption. This badly damaged Kenya's reputation as a politically stable country. The United Nations was called in to resolve the issue, and it was decided that the different political parties should share the power, although Kibaki would remain the president.

▶ *Kenyans line up patiently to vote in the 2007 elections. Everyone over the age of 18 can vote in Kenya.*

GOING GLOBAL

Kenya has played an important role in bringing peace to other countries, especially war-torn African countries. Kenya is one of the 12 countries that account for 75 percent of the total UN forces. In 2005, it helped bring an end to a civil war in Sudan, and it has helped prevent fighting in Somalia from spreading across the border. Kenyan troops and police have also served in Liberia and Sierra Leone.

Human Rights

When Daniel arap Moi was president, Kenya did not have a reputation as a leader in good human rights. People who criticized the government were often arrested, held without trial, and tortured. Other countries, especially those that gave Kenya aid, stopped sending money and refused to deal with the Kenyan government. Since Mwai Kibaki came to power in 2002, things have improved considerably, and in 2003, the Kenya National Human Rights Commission was set up to ensure that international human rights standards were met. However, major concerns with corruption in the police force remain.

▼ *A Kenyan peacekeeping soldier on a mission in Eritrea in northeast Africa. UN peacekeeping forces can be recognized by their blue helmets.*

Kenya has the potential to be a stable and successful country. To achieve this, it must continue to work closely with other countries to help build its economy. With a strong economy, all Kenyans may benefit and be able to improve their standards of living.

IT'S A FACT!

Vision 2030 is a plan for Kenya's economy over the next 20 years. Money will be spent developing areas such as tourism, farming, and information technology. Part of Vision 2030 is a bid for Kenya to host the Olympic Games in 2028.

Ethnic Conflicts

Differences and conflict between the ethnic groups are threatening Kenya's political stability. If there is more unrest, the tourist industry could suffer further, as people will be afraid to visit Kenya. Global events that Kenya may have no control over, such as terrorist incidents or global diseases that stop travel, could also affect the tourist industry.

▼ *Tourists come to see tribes such as the Maasai living their traditional ways. But what will happen if tourists are afraid of political instability?*

Local Government

Some people in Kenya think that local governments should have more power. They believe this would stop corruption in the higher levels of government as well as conflict between the different tribal groups. This system in Kenya is called *majimbo*. In the future, the commissioners of the Kenyan provinces may find they have more control over how their areas are run and over issues such as education and healthcare. However, there are those who argue that if the power of the main government is weakened, it may be harder to control events.

▲ *Kenyans celebrate the election of Barack Obama as U.S. president. Many believe that Kenya will benefit in some way from this.*

International Cooperation

Kenya's economic future could also lie in the development of the East African Community. Kenya is a key member of this organization, which encourages members to work together in the areas of politics and economics. This would create more trade and could lead to a common system of money and political unity. With more than 50 percent of Kenyans living on less than US$1 a day, battling poverty must remain a priority for the future.

Glossary

cash crops crops that are grown especially to be exported to other countries.

Christianity a religion that follows the teachings of Jesus Christ.

civil war when groups of people within a country fight one another.

continent one of the Earth's seven great land masses; Africa, Asia, Australia, Europe, North America, South America and Antarctica are continents.

coral reefs underwater structures formed from the remains and skeletons of sea creatures.

economy the financial system of a country or region, including how much money is made from the production and sale of goods and services.

equator an imaginary circle around the earth that divides it into northern and southern hemispheres.

ethnic group a group of people who identify with each other and feel they share a history.

export to transport products or materials abroad for sale or trade.

GDP gross domestic product; the total value of all goods and services produced in a country in a given year.

Islam a religion with belief in one god (Allah) and his last prophet, Muhammad.

Mau Mau a secret society of Kikuyus that led a rebellion against the ruling Europeans in Kenya in the 1950s.

migrate to move from one place to another.

Muslim someone who follows the religion of Islam.

nomadic roaming from place to place.

plateau a raised area of flat land.

pollution ruining the environment with man-made waste such as vehicle emissions, waste gases from factories, or chemicals from fertilizers.

rebellion an organized resistance to a government.

refugee someone who flees from war, oppression, or persecution in search of refuge and safety.

republic a form of government in which a country is ruled not by a king or queen, but by officials elected by the people.

rural relating to the countryside.

safari a Swahili word meaning "a trip"—usually referring to an overland journey to look for wildlife.

urban something that is related to or located in a city.

Further Information

Books

Kenya
Changing World
by Tish Farrell
(Arcturus Pub, 2011)

Kenya : a Question and Answer Book
Questions and Answers: Countries
by Sara Louise Kras
(Capstone Press, 2007)

Kenya
Country Explorers
by Sean McCollum
(Lerner Publications, 2008)

Living in Kenya
Living In
by Ruth Thomson
(Sea-to-Sea Pub, 2006)

Web Sites

http://www.oxfam.org.uk/coolplanet/kidsweb/world/kenya/index.htm
Oxfam's "Cool Planet" page on Kenya, with all sorts of information about the history, geography, and people of the country.

http://www.globaleye.org.uk/primary_spring01/focuson/kenya.html
The effects of tourism on Kenya.

http://www.tourism.go.ke
The official website of Kenya's Ministry of Tourism.

Every effort has been made by the publisher to ensure that these web sites contain no inappropriate or offensive material. However, because of the nature of the Internet, it is impossible to guarantee that the content of these sites will not be altered. We strongly advise that Internet access is supervised by a responsible adult.

Index

Numbers in **bold** indicate pictures